THE

OPEN SECRET

THE

OPEN SECRET

JENNIFER MOXLEY

FLOOD EDITIONS

CHICAGO

COPYRIGHT © 2014 BY JENNIFER MOXLEY

ALL RIGHTS RESERVED

PUBLISHED BY FLOOD EDITIONS

WWW.FLOODEDITIONS.COM

ISBN 978-0-9838893-9-7

COVER PHOTOGRAPH BY HAROLD GEE

DESIGN AND COMPOSITION BY QUEMADURA

PRINTED ON ACID-FREE, RECYCLED PAPER

IN THE UNITED STATES OF AMERICA

THIS BOOK WAS MADE POSSIBLE IN PART THROUGH

A GRANT FROM THE ILLINOIS ARTS COUNCIL

A poem is news of an other life.

ROBERT DUNCAN

THE

OPEN SECRET

THERE IS A BIRDSONG AT THE ROOT OF POETRY

FOR ANN LAUTERBACH

Hemmed in by an un-
tenable image:

     feathers planted

below fragile branches

     of avian feet   scaly crossroads scoring

a particular blue of sky

     offending

through the uselessness of misplaced

     forms   thorny prongs

that make no sense (and yet belong)

     on the ground

out of which

     the bird wings stiffly jut

rigid as

     rhubarb leaf.

          Should you

kneel the body's aged mechanism

     beneath the shade of dry feathers,

          should you

angle the vulnerable cavern

     of ear—trembling passage to psyche's

     failures   our fall

into suffering   knowledge—toward the root

          should you

listen   you *will* hear

1

the wasted strains of an underground song

rising from the muffled beak: site of a perverse smothering

throated core submerged

deadened by thoughtless depths

but alive

for the dead have kept it

safe from false music

a ghoulish guard of LOVE

SAFE from

Psyche

she who

bullied by the cruelty of others

the sophistication of fashionable libraries

the envy of those

who would molest the world into false confessions

and banish   all mystery

with their dripping

candles   she who would

unearth the birdsong   to cage it

she who   will end by destroying what she loves most.

Shhhh, quiet

listen:

it is drawn by other amblers

its strains awake in our attentions

as a sudden   bewildering   happiness

ear wedded to earth, listen

and hear

what those who know all

can not.

A FOOLISH CONSISTENCY

There is a fine reversal of desire
        that subtly turns to face
the wake of years hard spent
        refining taste,
reading this but never that, learning to
        discriminate
against the prejudice of time, at first,
        but later in ad-
herence to its
        logic.
Discrimination
        narrows
options,
        about which we are
breathless in our youth, when time is an
        endless, omniscient thing
just beyond the ego—toxic mercury
        bolting from undisciplined
voracious hungers.
        When I was young
I courted
        the unfathomable permanence
of books. Back then, before the internet, they were
        so difficult to find. And seemed a miracle.
        Especially rare, neglected books
        of rare, neglected knowledge.

The spiked-up enthusiasms of the gung-ho

        are easily winded

when shapeless. Life and death insights

        in the classroom

vanish

        when pedaling home

with thoughts of food, a favorite show,

        a stiff tag

scratching the skin

        of your infant

neck. No idea could compete

        until I fell

in love

        with work. The painful shaping

        of discrimination

kept that love at bay. I was afraid

        to write a thing I did not mean, and knew not what I meant.

        Underneath the ego's needs

an unsuspected

        truth

awaits, which all unfixed I went towards

        through composition's problems. Discrimination told me

        poetry could solve them.

A few wrong loves along the way

        have all but been

forgotten, shed

        in the refinement

of belief. A fine reversal

        of desire

has taken shape. Its genesis erased.

        I can't look back

or forward, and though

        I'm still misled

        by love, it doesn't feel

like love

        at all, but just

        a vague sensation

of what was once not

        and now

        is.

THE LONGING FOR SOMETHING TO PROTECT

ties us up with useless sorrow,
winds the intestinal spool
with a painful inept thread
spun of mercenary grief
       (the risk cop in our brain)

something to worry over
under our noses, in the way,
something to keep beside us
which cannot survive without us

something to go home for
and begrudge a little, a gentle
but not binding lease on this
supposedly commodious freedom
       (we check messages like addicts)

something to direct the directionless
heart and spin time's cottony mass
into something other than lists of tasks
       (the work will never be done)

something we cannot pay to insure
but without which we cannot live,
something that will be
       (though we won't see it)
indispensable to love's memory

LULLABY

Had I had children along the way,
two boys, a girl, the perfect three,
wouldn't they have played the games
I see the children across the street play
in the backyard and driveway of their
parents' house: classic, old-time games,
the games I played all day in the pebbly
alleyway behind my parents' house:
hopscotch, hula hoop, jump rope, and tag?

Wouldn't they have been hesitant
to put an end to it, to come in for the
evening and eat the meal I had cooked?
They would not hear the words
of our adult talk, kicking each other
under the table, confronting the task
of the food-filled plate before the gaze
of the overseer. After dinner, my children,
snapped back into the set agenda
of adult time, would make a bid
to postpone the inevitable with shared
entertainments (better than none).

But I would only think of money
and time's loss. I would, having felt
lonely all day long, long to be alone.
High-minded and with proper stiffness

I would send them by turns into
the baffling isolation of their own
rooms. They would resist, for my
children would know that once
in the exile of that artificial darkness
their infantile pleas for compassion
would be silenced by the paralysis
of obedience and sounds that loom.

But wouldn't my children be able
to quiet their fears without me,
focusing their attention on the
near-to-hand—the faintly lit
clock, the rumpled pattern
of the sheet, and so on? In silent
talk they'd learn their thoughts
and speak to the things beside them.

Then, fingers tapping a little charm
to fend off nightly evils, my children
would work quickly to lock their
secret inventory into future memory
before kidnapped by sleep.

ANNIVERSARY

No time to
write my
tribute
to the absent
inter-
locutor.
What a bureau-
cratic-sounding
word, yes, and
slightly hostile.
How about
confidante,
that's more intimate
though not quite
true. There was
so much
I didn't
tell you. You
were the backdrop
against which I
had a unique
value—a kind
smile of total
approval, or
its opposite—
to make me
crumple. I'm

due for a crown.
The gray silver
filling has dimmed
the thinning
enamel of an
old tooth. A
bicuspid? Who knows,
I've never known
the names of
teeth, except for
those I've lost—
wisdom. This one,
on the upper
right, can
no longer
hold it-
self together.
If nothing is done
to prop it up,
there's an empty gap
in my future. Twenty years
without you.
Like air—so pillowy
in memory—
whistling painfully
through what's
missing. What
we can't get
used to.

NO PLACE LIKE

Never a prophet at the curb
of what was once called "home"
insidious   *word*   prohibition.

Never a prophet in the adopted land
ill-fitting into   the familiar
wandering among signposts and lawns,
dreaming   of the lost Eden   touched—
trying to find the insidious   *word*   and warmth
like loyal Lassie risking her life by swimming the rushing Tweed:
half-dead, mud-drenched, and bone-tired, a dog fugitive
from booted cruelty, whips, and chains, lying flat beside the rustic cottage
for the kindly old couple to find.
          Would that Dame May Whitty lived
behind this row of shut doors (they lie you know)
          down Main Street   hoping to share
                    her milky ration, a methodical brushing
and words: soothing, sweet   oft-repeated   there *there*.

When in Rome, Berlioz thought only of Paris
though she had jilted him and wrote to say so.
When he crossed the border the masters gathered
to wave their hands   "good riddance"   keep your exhausting brilliance
                    at a handsome distance.

Born in the south, he chose the city that bespoke his *Symphonie Fantastique*
streets to match the grandeur

of a young man's extravagant enterprise

but instead of praise he was greeted with

paranoia   *silence*   *brutal confusion.*

When in Paris, I thought only of you

      "sitting in a park," etc.   the warmth of the sun

on black tights, palm knowledge

      in Balboa Park,

longing for the comfort of a known address

      stenciled on the curbside.

But all my blood ties were by that time undone, and I could not return

except   by resumé   and failed   unloved

or so it felt, by what refused me in its history.

Scenes in which our memories are set resist us with their silence.

Better not to seek them out   better to stay away   there is an

      uncanny sadness

that comes from driving through memorized streets

      with no hope of seeing someone you know,

the incognito

      of long absence, a stranger in a land that is *not* strange

surrounded by ghosts who tempt your sanity with their silhouette feet.

Once it was you who walked the borders of these ant-filled cracks: *launched fairy dreams,*

stains, a massacre or two . . .

The intimacy of sidewalks embarrasses,

though there's been no angelic change it is *as if* you never existed *as if*   Lassie finally made it back only to find the cottage

                              crumbling, the boy taken

moldering in an unmarked grave   No, that's not it

It is *as if*

            Lassie finally made it back but turned out to be mistaken,

                 there never had been a cottage   or a boy

only a desolate mangy stray's invented dream of welcome

                everything risked for the imagined hearth.

We can remember where we put our things and still manage to lose them.

Berlioz, loved not in Paris,

            resented for offering a brightness to match the great cities—

                which turn small town when confronted with genius,

            abuse their need for sure bets,

                want the momentous after the fact.

Me, out of place on a beach, at home at sunset, asleep in a room

            I've rented

                  unknown   both *here*   and there, *there.*

COASTAL

FOR MONIQUE VAN GENDEREN

I

Your lover claimed that in Los Angeles nothing felt changed.

And now? As California melts down with wildfires

and fiscal crises I feel irritated at its dominance.

Hogging the airwaves and votes. "It's like a war out there,"

you wrote, speaking not of the budget shortfall

but of being an "old" artist in a young business.

"But we're only middle-aged," I thought,

an unromantic stage. Today the sky is the color

of Henry Fonda's eyes, bright, crisp, and principled.

As if no time had passed, or as if the same September sky

from eight years ago this day decided to reappear.

       That morning (which feels both far and near)

I walked with a red-faced blond

from a climate-controlled classroom

across the grass to the airless environment

of Neville Hall. Cinderblock walls, vinyl floors,

and damaged acoustical ceiling tiles stained

with yellow-brown spots.

       Caedmon was in my ear:

"Now let us praise heaven-kingdom's Guardian

the Measurer's might and his mind-plans . . ."

A partially opened office door cast light geometry on the floor.

Steve was on the phone with my brother,

atypically calling from San Francisco at eleven in the morning.

Gesturing he mouthed the words. "A plane, etc."

and then the no-way-back expression

of gradual understanding slowly edged with dread.

One minute, two minutes, three minutes, four.

How long does it take to know

what is not lived but told?

        Perched on a chair, the breath re-calibrates,

detailed questions begin. The image: a bi-plane

leaving an I-beam, disabused by a small

black-and-white TV atop a file cabinet in the lounge.

The "two tours" Vietnam vet, hired to teach

composition, raging through the hall,

thrilling with the fear that he might be called

back to active duty. I hadn't seen such fierceness in him

since his can of strawberry Slim Fast

went missing from the communal fridge.

The hungry turn bestial, roar against reason.

        After depositing my bag in Steve's office

we left the stifling building. It was a beautiful day.

Incredibly beautiful, exactly like today, or like

those days I had in abundance growing up

in California—cool, crisp mornings, warming to

seventy degrees. A breeze with a slight chill to it,

if you are sitting still in shade. Classes

were cancelled for the remainder of the day.

        On the way out a man passed us

cackling and shouting, "This is absurd!"

A disquisition quite distinct from the worried
and quiet acknowledgment we met in most
faces. His "You're all fools!" echoed loudly
as he charged toward the fire doors,
a woman nodding behind him,
hurrying to keep apace.
                    The world seemed mute, a backdrop,
too perfect. Chickadee chirps echoed against it
but seemed as fake as a nature tape loop. We could not
hear them, blocked by the loud buzz of what ifs,
the deafening hum of the stunned structure,
the "me" of belief underneath our feet
yoked into the juggernaut "we."

                              II

"It was like it was just something on TV,"
your lover said. "We watched the news
in disbelief, but then life went on as usual."
The usual of two women caught up
in the L.A. art world. It was only a few months
before this that I had sat across a table from you
sipping the honey-peach of a rich Sauternes,
so jet-lagged and mastered by valium
that everything seemed a dream. The next
morning, sitting amidst the eucalyptus debris
of your tiny backyard, I was lulled by the
incredible warmth. I thought the sun could burn away

the entirety of my existence, stunned as I was
by the surreality of being so thoughtlessly content.
        After the "war" you also wrote:
"The other night my friend had a party.
There was skateboarding in someone's studio
on a homebuilt ramp. After many cocktails I have
quite a few wounds." It would have sounded incredible
had I not walked the gala galleries of the superrich
in your company. But this isn't right. I have
edited out the freeway deadfall, the sound barriers beneath
the brown haze. Vignettes of contrast serve self-pity,
a cock-tease to the happiness contract
I am always promising to honor if somebody, not me,
makes everything change. Besides, I'm exaggerating.
Your studio is a dark garage down a canyon road
lit by artificial light. We are trying, the both of us,
to make work that matters. To remain true
to that initial commitment. Artifice, dialogue, beauty.
A letter to a friend. "This glamorless isolation is killing me."
I cannot accompany you into the abstract,
but grow more narrative by the year,
saying things to get them said,
feeling no leisure to take old risks.

                        III

Episodes. The drizzle demands a change of plan.
No day, no hour, not even a second can be

adequately written in one sitting. The occasion
is over, but the poem continues. Keys fly but
the chore of recording the "facts" still fails the story.
What description can match that fraction
of morning consciousness that floats free of identity—
these past few days it has been occupied by Jo
returned to shatter my nebulous pleasure
and fill the gap with a fetal cramp, impulsive, wet,
and infantile. I want to be cared for *in that way*,
to bury my head in her polyester lap, to risk
her impatience with my half-baked adulthood.
An elegant maturity without responsibility.
The babyhood of ladies. I remember the letter
in which you expressed your anger at those
who deigned to hoard parents,
to stay untroubled by death.

          There is such a light out,
gray brightness, gold-leaf storm clouds
to excite the wardrobe, deepen the green of the pines.
The desert offers no such options, even
when millions of gallons of water are piped in
from distant rivers. This morning I envy you
a broad material surface on which to really
stretch out. The tangible space you press against.
My words will not reflect the sun, nor conjure
watery moods, not here in this study. A study is not
like a studio. It is a cramped place filled with the mind's
idiosyncratic props. Visitors are not welcome.
A studio invites everyone in. Made things

unabashedly court flirtatious comment,

proud to be "in progress."

       Have eight years sunk down in the furniture?

Settled in winter, age, the ways. The initial impulse

having become the plodding pleasures of vocation,

always so difficult to share. "Poetry is a team sport,

you cannot play it alone," to quote the great poet

of company—a beautiful embellishment of fellowship,

or the acknowledgment that all of our words come

from the very same store. Whether multinational

or a dinner invite I think of company as something

you work for. In its absence I cling to its promises

with a childlike faith in mutual understanding,

when in fact, even in childhood, one kid was

always the boss. Once your belief in humanity vanishes

all time becomes borrowed, the slightest freedom "luck."

Is *privilege*, therefore, the surreptitious mission

and final end of human rights?

       "The poem should not ask such questions,"

chirps the goldfinch from the window. Plumage is all.

Like your canvas colors—yellows, blacks, and grays,

suggesting an abstract flower, a record of your gestures.

I edit the pulse of my mind. Distraction dominates me.

Even the punctured shimmer of a revelation

needs at least an afternoon to become established.

Things must be shaped by thought to matter.

I have written this all before. A fine-dust fear settled

that day and stifled the demands. No more

face-to-face. Now, out in California, the professors

are getting angry. Not about the war, which,

for those of us not directly involved, seems to have

faded into a sort of brutal Muzak murmuring

in the distance. The professors are mad

about pay cuts. Will the "regents" bankrupt

the one tier of education California is good at?

As unreal to me as the bi-sexual Berkeley orgy,

the nubile soup I have been reading about

in agonized letters from West Coast friends, I think:

I envy those University of California professors.

Here in Maine we are paid . . . but wait,

"this is boring," says the kitten, leaving a string

at my feet. Motivation should come from

the quest, you know, the one infused with

wrenching nostalgia and the loss of all your friends.

Nothing like a piece of string to focus the attention.

Or a line of poetry, snaking down the length of the page

tempting me to taste the sweetness of the body's

pulse and risk expulsion from this moment

into a fogged sprint toward a sheer drop.

Clarity of vision is the gift you get

once you have started to fall.

IV

The option to refresh existence by

returning to patterns established in youth

bores me. Youth bores me. I cannot be excited

by watching others learn things for the first time.
And the thing is, there really is no "first time"
in learning. Like flimsy paper register receipts
on windy supermarket parking lots,
revelations rest for only a second before
being whisked off for good. What seemed so crucial
when first grasped is just as quickly forgotten.
I know (unscientifically) that many of my ideas
tried to get in for many years before I actually let them.
This did not happen out of stubbornness, but out of
a misplaced loyalty to a past I was always catching up with.
Defending defunct ideas that changed me as though
they were people in the room I might
unwittingly offend.

       I do not want to go back to the beginning,
to that litany of shameful moments
and unearned self-assurance. The bluster
of an attitude, flesh quivering with chaotic
feeling. I am glad that phase is over.
"No you're not," says Humpty Dumpty
sitting soiled on the shelf, acting the Renaissance
egg. So then, shall I be reawakened, like a British
spinster in the overdone plotline whose clit
is coaxed out of hiding by some swarthy
peasant while she's "on holiday"? The trajectory
is as follows: unedited youth moves to gradual
repression, with one final bounce back,
then reconciliation with the aging lover
you thought a stranger until you realize

that he is your "best friend." But it is all a lie. Men trade in

for new models, and why not, the rates are good,

and though others click their tongues, secretly

they are impressed. Some even call it love.

What they do not tell you is that the slow warming

of the same body over the same flame for many years

is the more various option, not the less. It is easier

to hit repeat and go back to the start than to find yourself

in the middle for the very first time. "The old are new to age,"

and so on, as it says in the famous poem. And how

are you faring in your relationship? Monogamous bliss?

Lesbian sex death? Or a life of high-drama French-style affairs?

The little of your history I know leads me to think

the latter. But then again, those who knew me

"when" would probably think the same.

And it's not true. I'm not blue, just groping for examples.

"At your age"? I know. But I grew up in a youth-obsessed

region of a youth-obsessed culture, and so I lost some time.

        The late sixties and early seventies flipped

everything around. They banned the hats and gloves

once used to hide aged pates and liver spots,

exposing adults as the affronts they are to the illusion of

eternal youth. The Southern California sidewalks

swarm with the surgically altered, dressed like children

twenty-four seven in brightly colored clothes,

walking ads for corporate aestheticism

masquerading as personal taste. Here in New England

it is an offense to God to think about your looks.

Try it and winter—Protestantism's greatest ally—

will take you down a notch. Nineteenth-century loggers
defied the weather and turned to the noble white pine
to say, "Hey babe, looking good." They then felled
the beauty's self, and left us only guessing.

V

Berkeley's nostalgia for its protest past
trumps So-Cal, where only a few professors
laid down their pointers and headed out to the surf.
The recession is not turning out to be "great"
nor the protests more than symbolic.
Poems in recent journals have forgotten
there's a world. That's a new trick:
to leave the world out yet still be "political."
Picasso painted hundreds of portraits of the artist
and none resembled him in the least. His alter ego
was bearded and skinny with too long a torso,
far from the round brown grandpa type
mid-century delighted in thinking the icon
of childlike painterly genius. You are a play
of the eye, delineating an aesthetic pleasure
located in color's relief, the effort you put in a
temporary installation a nod to the primacy
of making, a thumb at market value.
We all want to be valued, but not by false markers
used to placate the ignorant scions of clarity—or people
who can only love what they do not have to defend.

A muggy sunny day, better for plants

than people. As the poem travels through time

the anniversaries shift. It has been a year since

men and women in dark blue suits

left tall office buildings carrying cardboard boxes.

Bankers on parade. The perversity of virtual lives

made real by exposure. If no one finds out

that you broke the law then are you really culpable?

The Woody Allen school of morality. The above lines betray

a morning with Rae, her scissored lines the best cure

for my retrograde romanticism. She has flown to Maine from

my hometown to give a poetry reading. "Your house

is nicer than mine," she says, exhibiting her chronic

(self-diagnosed) divulging of the truth. "But, then again,"

she continues, "mine is in California."

VI

How would you like the politics in your poetry?

How about in your painting? Romantic and sad

or smart and structural? Whatever your answer

you will leave here thinking you've done

a little something for the good of mankind.

BUT IN THIS CASE YOU'D BE WRONG!

"Oh preachy," says the pencil sharpener,

with its genuine claim to making points, "for the last time

the name of the game is NAMING, not explaining."

Presenting the world whole in its overwhelming beauty
from the vantage point of your sidelined authority.
Anniversaries, as the poem was saying: TARP, my
mother's birthday, Vladimir Horowitz, exiled
and in the closet, surrounding his piano with strong
marines. Every day is worth marking for something,
though few can agree on what.

       Feeling panicky about going on so long I show
this to Steve in draft form. "So this is your 9/11 poem?"
Echoes of an oft-quoted line from *Reds*:
"With all that's going on in the world" . . . Why now?
Because my older brother hasn't called me for months,
as if inflated Bay Area real estate has swallowed him
for good, because my little brother is locked up
with hep-C and the California prison system
too bankrupt to pay for health care. I don't know.
There are reasons, but these are not them.

       It was just a train of thought. That started it.
It was the fault of that beautiful sunny day,
and me sitting out on the closed-in porch. Suddenly
I was wistful for those endless gentle mornings
on the back steps of my home state, that
head-in-the-sand on the edge of time.
A train of thought about a trainless state,
though I've just heard that the Golden Bear
is making a grab for the bulk of government money
set aside for high-speed rails. The hog that squandered
its own economy hollering for more. How I long for you.

Yet whenever I go back home, Fate, the bully,

yells at me with the same old story: "You must take

this surfboard and walk east until someone

mistakes it for a canoe." Boo hoo.

VII

In school I was told that poems only matter

if rooted in the landscape. A baffling decree for an abstract

art. At least you could *sculpt*, if you really had to.

I wrote about a sidewalk with a false sense of history.

A Seven-Eleven and a chainlink fence. That

was the past. Since moving to the outer edge

of the almost forgotten I have developed a loathing

for the pride of regions. The local wants to distract you

into forgetting that there is a world. "I won't,"

I say, "I won't," stamping my feet in place.

As payback for my loathing of small ponds

I have been diagnosed with this one: "sarcoidosis"

the doctor says, a disease that clusters

in central Maine. So now we both live in places

that can cause our lungs irreparable harm.

I think of Eva Hesse breathing in her resin,

or Rothko sopping walls with cheap gallons

of hardware-store paint. The off-gassing

from your vinyl strips seeping into the lobby fabrics

of the Renaissance Hollywood Hotel. Strange

when cravings come, and will not stand for

substitutes. I get them for seeing art, not *virtually*
but in person. Online your paintings lose their gloss
to become as flat as these words, which can't even
manage to dent the page or bump along the fingers.
I cannot recall the feeling I get when looking
at art I love. I must return to face it. To stand
before it, to feel its effect. Like the longing for a food
you cannot reproduce. The patty melt, for example,
which is completely unknown in these parts.
Or so I discovered one frustrating day
when, seized by a craving, I made Steve drive me
from Denny's to Applebee's to T.G.I. Friday's
only to face dumbfounded looks from chubby hostesses
clutching full-color laminate menus. The ache
of a hunger for something you could once find
right down the street. Why do I go on?
Who cares that a middle-aged West Coast poet
living in New England is craving a patty melt.
"I'll make her pay," thinks my colon, plotting its revenge.
        I know to take it seriously. Something
about the fragility of existence came home to me
the evening of the day before my first procedure.
I was only forty-three, cheated of seven years
scopy-free living by nonchalantly passing blood.
What might this stand in for, *metaphorically*, I thought,
as I lay on the couch, forcing myself to eat lemon jello.
Schuyler pissing all over Paris had a kind of charm,
the little-boy-cum-blubbering-sweetheart, in love
with hunks and life, loses control on the Champs-

Élysées and we all feel a sense of relief. The poem
has told its story, has spent its epistolary passions
out of the loneliness of being trapped in a place
that is so far from all of your friends. An inelegant sense
of loss mixed with my gratitude for bourgeois privacy
when I downed the two-week dose of Fleet enema
in a few short hours. The sensation was like
gagging on seawater, or like all of the saliva
of prehistory being concentrated in your mouth.
When the body's content empties out,
the "you" of convictions no longer exists. The poet
of cultivated mystique denied identity's protection
is just another sick person in a hospital bracelet
grateful to take orders. Gradually I lost my self
in this nightmare (which was a childhood fear).
As the hours of the arduous test progressed
I became more than usually media vulnerable,
and finally I all but vanished into the dubbed voices
and lawless cruelty of *Once Upon a Time in the West*.

BE CAREFUL: THE POET'S SKIN

IS LIKE THAT OF A FROG

There is a way in which
          I can be distracted
from what matters. Work
          and its allures: to make
another's woes your business,
          to seem busy and feel
the pleasant purpose of temporary urgencies.

          We walk away knowing what we will do
and then forget to do it. Interpose:
          a couch on which to doze awhile,
scenes of the once bright world
          drifting through the swirl
of the lazy, overfed mind.

          I have no illusions
regarding my accomplishments.
          Knowledge is not something
I am hoping to find, but feels rather
          like the wave-bumps beneath
the blue plastic of a too-soft waterbed.
          I feel awkward on it,
unable to orient or get up. Denied hard surety
          I am yet quite comfortable,

bobbing around atop half-fact like

    a giddy fool

who speaks her secrets to the moon

    the moment no one is looking.

    Meanwhile, some are holding forth.

Some seem to know

    what others will be impressed by.

Some have conviction,

    at least in public. Others quietly move along,

honoring the persuasions of their youth,

    lying to themselves. Some

await discovery, growing anxious

    with the years.

Others are afraid to tell you.

    The outside wants in,

the inside would like to be left alone

    to parse out its prerogatives

in soporific silence. The body provides

    all the form we need.

Me I'm falling asleep, not waiting for

    inspiration but for food

to court my interest and

    my mood to lift.

    I love the world in its wrongs

and do not feel equipped to solve them.

    Others strut solutions.

Go to it, I say, bored with the small-time
                  secular pulpit. Simplicity
will win my heart. (Tell this
                  to the balsa-wood bug
clinging to the screen door. His fragility
                  is a fleeting beauty
that portends destruction.)

                  Logics are demanded.
But wait awhile, listen, be quiet
                  and observe. Your mind
has become enamored of puzzling out
                  structure, it does not become
you, o poet! Who now will take
                  the wind's dictation,
atomize life into light, bring us
                  the meaning
and not the "explanation"?

                  Build instead of footnote,
history will take care of the rest.

R . I . P .

Not forced to fall for hideous Phaon,

nor to drift dreamlike from

a Victorian cliff, pursued by visions

of slender limbs, peach-soft hair,

dewy violets clustered

in an unwilling lap, not exiled

on a distant island for writing

smartly about love, not called amoral

nor forgotten, not murdered

by a jealous lover, nor weakened

from drink, did not make an incision

in the veins, never murdered

in a tavern at twenty-nine

nor thought mad, released immediately

from St. Luke's Hospital for Lunatics,

freed from Northampton

General Lunatic Asylum,

cured of syphilis, not mad

nor ruined by drink nor shot

in the head, the rope unknotted

and fluidly slid from the lamp-

post, sauntered away with a sideways

crawl up the Champs-Élysées,

never sickened from drink

nor drowned in the Gulf of Spezia,

the heart kept tight swam madly

toward shore, disappeared down

the glistening beach skipping

happily in the direction of England,

staved off fever while fighting

for Greeks, lived, wrote, erased

the blood-stained pillowcase, married Fanny,

moved to Finland, fathered several

pink-skinned children, lay down for a rest

in the Baltimore street, got up

confused about Spanish port and

went to the graveyard to sleep it off,

laudanum, opium, stroke, paralysis,

aphasia, angels, threads of exotic Delacroix

visions, but everything was put right

when mom said, "Come on home,

I want to care for you," left the house

and walked into the river until

the water level covered the hairline

then shed the heavy Edwardian garments

and broke into a birdlike breaststroke

exclaiming, "How lovely to be free

of the sickbed!" never destroyed by drink,

sang while removing the shrapnel from

a soldier, recovered from the Spanish flu,

returned to Poland all debts forgiven

by appreciative readers from the Congo,

replaced the bottle of Lysol among toxic

rats enjoying a sauna under the sink,

did not pull the trigger or push the chair

out from under the revolution

while screaming about the army of the arts,

put on a jacket and sailed to Mexico,

calmly came up on deck, folded

the jacket over the rail, and then—

arrested by a vision of spread-eagled sailors

descending like angels through

the turquoise sky—decided *not*

to swallow the sea, freed from Payne Whitney,

walked right on through the psychiatric

state hospital and out the other side,

had no psychotic break while on acid

in a land of dreamlike torch singers

masquerading as Satanists, never touched the stuff,

the dead liver tissue miraculously mended,

smoker's cough silenced, cured by the sea air

of old gray Gloucester, jumped into

the beach taxi and drove down the beach

gesticulating gaily toward the setting sun,

not undone, unloved, forgotten, nor

filled with despair, not punished for talking

with angels, not unhappy nor alone,

not misrepresented nor misunderstood

nor nauseous from drink or drugs or depression,

loved respected and read

long-lived healthy and happy

celebrated by all in life before

dying contented in a comfortable bed.

LISTEN

FOR KEITH WALDROP

Whenever I fear myself a bore
I think of listening. I should,
I tell myself, do it more.

I know a man who can give
more attention to his meal
than a room, yet still listen.

He looks suspiciously like Ruskin.

He does not boast. Yet if he recollects
an anecdote illustrative of human folly
a mischievous gleam inflects
his milky blue eyes, trailed by a little grin.

The failure of outlandish ploys
especially delights him.

He sometimes speaks about the Bible
as though he knows it start to end. He does.

Though he is neither pious nor dour.

When I sit near him I have a tendency
to chatter. Am I nervous or trying to amuse?
I am trying to set him off, in a friendly way.

To elicit the delicious state of listening:
I seek the open sesame, a magic word
that will joggle the charmed book
from off the shelf of his memory.

I will not have heard of it.
My naiveté, ever on offer, raises
his eyebrows. They are wiry and stiff.

He has given me gifts that bid me listen.
A ponderous boxed set of thickly cut
long-playing records, Bach's *St. Matthew Passion*.

Books, countless books, all freakishly apt.

Sometimes, when he's grumpy I find
I fear his judgment, though toward me
he has always been well-mannered and kind.

His conspicuous love of women
makes him a very poor curmudgeon.

He delights in strange stories. Tales that teeter
at the edge of incredible but nevertheless
are quite true. He likes to read bad meter,
and to share odd knowledge known to few.

He has his share in Adam's curse, although
he does not seem to. A gift for surface levity
props up this masquerade. Without pretense
or martyrdom the pages blow by gently.

Listen and you might hear them, chuckling.

NOT THAT, DISAPPOINTMENT

I am inappropriate   I feel it
in every said thing   in every
enthusiasm   desire   wish
but mostly in every
          unsettling ambition.

I live for the light in the dark
of history   the ease of accomplishments
          after the fact
(it will all seem inevitable, after the fact)
the irritable need to remove
          the disturbance
of how I am failing in so many ways
and   having lost myself and "their" values
the distance between you and me
          is abolished. Might I speak to you
in the quiet of your tower?
1571   "the reader replaces the dead"   1919
the dead speak to the writer   of ambitious verticality
a mind that prefers
                    conversation
with vanished spirits and the not yet living.

          When I think of it
I too would like to become a father   late in life
to awaken to the sweetly sour dewiness of infancy
dozing at the foot of my toasty bed

the room's vacancy
now filled with the emptiness of past bedrooms
would be filled with a child's potential
I would write poems to that potential
I would shut out the world and think only
of it   it would be a *literary* desire
a dream   not of structure   but of substance
we can play at structure   can play at it
build categories of welcome that yet remain empty
while substance becomes
a book   a desk   a library
the leisure to imagine that in talking to God
the whole of history might listen in.

There you are   against a beautiful backdrop
standing sober in velvet   holding a discarded book
aware of the cool air on your skin
oblivious to the forces
that would block your journey
if they knew the extent of your inappropriate ambition
(Baldwin in the Harlem stacks, raging against his stepfather).

A glorious resistance to a deadening system becomes you
down on your knees   resigned to embodying
a shattered sequence
of a broken soul in a broken tower
the dream of the child at the foot of the bed
asleep   that is
yourself

GRAY-EYED ATHENA

Dumb before the sign, we might wander for decades
lacking the words for things we mutely feel, living
without dreaming in the dreary present of flat moments.
Aghast at the practical shape life takes when threatened
by insecurity. No one can predict what tools you will need,
and those who waste what they are given will blame the gift
and spare you it. Such are the foibles that doom the
too quick generational shift.

             I was taught how to repeat what others say
and waste the day with dreams. I cannot live without
the sense that I am overcoming something. Boredom
perhaps. This language I stumble over, that language I long for,
the word that's still unlearned that might unlock the
door that blocks the thought to break the will which shrivels
in waiting not making.

             Words are not the compromise
I made because I could not sing. Writing is not a failure.
Reading does help. When Odysseus discovered
how endless days of ocean bore he began to embroider
the story, a pleasure so addictive he postponed
his homecoming.

             The Greeks were right: living forever
is not a matter of faith but fame. But not the empty
momentary fame of teenage fantasy, a narcissistic dream,
but the fame of erasure into the network of this word
next to that, of shaping the shapeless face of days into a tale
that looks and sounds surprisingly like your own, but isn't.

MOMENTS WITHOUT VISION

I do not detect the quiet before the north-facing window

Is opened, then the boom of a gearshift faced with an incline

Enters the sunny porch. "People and Products You Can Trust."

The thought is gone. The lingering of night's plummet

Promises the end of such dawns. Returning to the set up

My body recoils from the gelid plastic of the weatherproof chair.

The kitten crashes through packing paper chasing the artificial mouse.

Sleep has been forgotten, replaced by the fudged

Reconstruction of a dream. Attention rejects the obvious.

Longs to forget its needs. Hot tea, ordered especially, embitters.

The unconscious, addicted to the trick of significance, scours

The uninspiring vista for triggers to expand, accordion-like,

Any from the legion of paper-doll selves crumpled into memory.

No lingering taste to the blueberries, bananas, and yoghurt

Confronting the palate. Then an unpleasantness. A tiny stem,

Not tasted as lime green but seen. The shudder of the unexpected thing

Entering the mouth. The regret. What this diary accomplishes.

The now into recognized patterns, description in order to see.

Relief from the need to keep saying: what remains outside these pages.

I read her desire, desire its pulse, then look beyond the window to the street.

People are going to work, jogging, walking dogs, walking for health,

Biking in spandex and helmets. I reject my connection to them

And think: there is no vision in visible purpose. I would return

To London, 1926. To an isolated writer recording her guilt
At wasting time with a diary. It is an avoidance of "life" and "work,"
Made smooth within the ink of it. Imported purpose into this
Moment in which there is seemingly none.

                                        I am assuaged
By the news that another self turned uncomfortably in place,
No matter the surrounding glamour, the legions of famous friends.
The water closet is cold, the world a seductive irritant, a thin
Liquid that drowns you in its indifference to your love of it.

WHAT WAS IT?

I was eating my dinner alone,
sitting on the living-room couch
watching a movie on TV for company
when the forces your covetous presence prevents
slowly crawled out in fibrous droves.

Without you to follow me with your
clipboard, or record the game my face plays,
masquerading as a cryptic territory
and your field of study, the energy maggots
turned the furniture into an ectoplasmic
mass with the weight of iron: soft but
resistant, a taut balloon against the hand.

Hypnotized by the atmosphere I fell asleep,
and the chair took revenge on my psyche.
I could not scream, so I focused my will
on pushing back against the animate matter.
I was near failing when I managed to utter
the word "dove," and then you shook me awake.

"Stop," stop fighting with the furniture, you said.
Yet something I could not see pushed hard
against me, and it was not a force for good.
My vocal chords were paralyzed and the language
of the living was the only way to stop it.

THIEVES

The soaked crow beside the road
has lost his definition. His smooth
bird outline and shiny blue-black
feathers—once used by poets
to describe the color of
their beloved's hair—
are dulled and dripping. He seems
attired in unkempt fur, wooly.
Like a yak. His stick legs gingerly
step beneath him through a muddy
puddle. The surrounding neon grass
plays its role as the gatekeeper
of the busy college road, lying
obedient before the digital clock
in the yard of the national bank's
prim and well-kept local branch.

DISCREPANT RESOLVE

At dusk Tinker's Island became suddenly
dramatically gilded (is that the word?),
lit against the slate-blue Atlantic,
accompanied by glistening small boats.
The whole scene was grotesquely picturesque,
arresting. How might Elizabeth Bishop
describe this, I wonder, not then as I watched,
but now as I write. Then I didn't think. I watched.
Ignoring the company to attend to the beauty.

Driving home after dinner I brooded
that this was not my vista, nor ever would
be, for I had not the energy nor will
to obtain it. A dream house built by a
couple in their second marriage near the
end of life. What hope, I thought, what faith!

DIVIDEND OF THE SOCIAL OPT OUT

How lovely it is not to go. To suddenly take ill.
Not seriously ill, just a little under the weather.
To feel slightly peaked, indisposed. Plagued by
a vague ache, or a slight inexplicable chill.

Perhaps such pleasures are denied
to those who never feel obliged. If there are such.

How pleasant to convey your regrets. To feel sincerely
sorry, but secretly pleased to send them on their way
without you. To entrust your good wishes to others.
To spare the equivocal its inevitable rise.

How nice not to hope that something will happen,
but to lie on the couch with a book, hoping that
nothing will. To hear the wood creak and to think.
It is lovely to stay without wanting to leave.

How delicious not to care how you look,
clean and uncombed in the sheets. To sip
brisk mineral water, to take small bites
off crisp Saltines. To leave some on the plate.

To fear no repercussions. Nor dodge
the unkind person you bug.

Even the caretaker has gone to the party.
If you want something you will have to
get it yourself. The blue of the room seduces.
The cars of the occupied sound the wet road.

You indulge in a moment of sadness, make
a frown at the notion you won't be missed.
This is what it is. You have opted to be
forgotten so that your thoughts might live.

THE CRIME OF APPETITE

FOR M. F. K. FISHER'S HUNGER

Hungers that arise out of happiness
lessen the breath, burst into laughter.
They sigh decidedly then sob, they crabbily
kick against contentment. They ask the
shame-baked ego to explain its cheap
obedience to fate. Food helps, but
only if eaten slowly and in smallish
portions. a treat one half of half the gift
of everything you've ever dreamed of.
Girls who push their plates away admit
they have no future, denying life's few
pleasures as if to say: *so there!* Close-
fisted, tasteless, and mean, they risk no
influence.

       First times, though rare, cannot
be provoked by questing after exotic tastes.
Hungers that arise out of happiness
shred quotidian pleasures. Undermine
experience, explain our fondness for
privation to our hatred of denial. There
is more up ahead, but you must choose
wisely. Settling in the dust of things
looking for the lost delight of dramatic
expectations. Anything to make

this acquisitive triumph taste less like
what you always wanted. There's got to be
more to this art of wanting what you have,
a glass of wine, a salad, a perfectly cooked
soft-boiled egg broken over buttered toast.
A window to look out of. Or, even better,
the thought of an old hunger, savored
if not quite satisfied, the boast of no
regrets and the present of a famished soul
who understands no thievery in aching
daily for the honest appetites at hand.

EVACUATIONS

The present is resistance, punctured every third day
by a minor enthusiasm. The possibility of a new coat.
The seesaw of desire for a new coat. Thoughts
of how stylish a new coat would be. Disappointment
at the fact that there is no one in the region
you want to impress with a stylish new coat.
The mental rehearsal of the passive-aggressive
comments about your inappropriate stylishness.
Thoughts of how much money you could save
by not buying a new coat. Of how much cheaper
it would be to dry-clean the coat you bought
three years ago, which is fine, but has a pink
lipstick stain on the edge of its brushed-wool
putty-colored sleeve. The feeling of strange pleasure
that comes when you deny yourself little
temporary desires. The strange pleasure
of giving in to buying new things. Of laying
them on the clean puffiness of the white comforter
in the bedroom. Of cutting off their tags
and security devices. Their newness.
Their failure to compensate for the fact
that you don't really want to go anywhere
in the region, even when dressed in a new thing
that looks crisp but isn't yet quite comfortable.

The present is resistance, punctured every third day
by a minor enthusiasm. The anticipation of a really

delicious steak. A filet mignon. The turning over
in the mind of all the different preparations of filet
mignon. How unadventurous. The desire to find
a new, better, more up-to-date preparation for filet
mignon. Chipotle, say. Or, the desire to be an
historically grounded person unmoved by fashion
who cooks filet mignon according to the great chefs
of the past. The best way. Unadorned. Well-seared.
With *beurre maître d'hôtel*. Thoughts of what a life
that included *beurre maître d'hôtel* on a daily basis
would be like. Wondering if there ever was such a life.
Thoughts of disappointment. No matter how tasty
the filet mignon, or what preparation you choose,
the satisfaction and elegance of it will no doubt
throw into relief all that is not elegant about the present.
The way in which the present is best when thinking
about the past. Not necessarily your own past,
but any past. In other words, reading. Or listening
to music. But books are always about first times
and music, too, is often about the first time you
heard it. Before it has become yours, but when you
already desire it to be so. The first stanza always wants
the second stanza to be just like it. The poet starts
counting in order to show the "active" reader
that counting is intentional and structure meaningful,
and both are true. Repetition is also a convenient device.
If I just repeat things, people will take note. If I think
about the past my life will seem to have a kind of
structure. But sometimes you need a new recipe.

My feet are cold in the present. Then they are hot.

In shoes indoors they become sweaty and then

outside they are hot, wet, and cold all at once.

When, at the end of the workday I take off my

vinyl boots I then must "unstick" my thin lady

socks from my feet. The two seem to have become one.

As you see, feet are very present. When I think about the past,

I never think about feet. But I do remember some

shoes that I kept on wearing even though they

hurt a lot. Not because I am a masochist, I'm not,

but because they conformed to an idea I couldn't

let go of, even when it caused me pain. Now that

I see that feet are connected to ideas perhaps I should

think more about them in the past. But I am not

going to think about the past anymore,

so feet in the past are definitely out. My feet

are sometimes blue, because I have Raynaud's syndrome.

Or so my brother told me one day when he was

standing in an inch of hot water in a bathtub

trying to warm his feet. He has Raynaud's syndrome

too. But that is a story from the past,

which is irrelevant. My brother is not in the present.

I am always having to pee in the present. I am always

also drinking fluids. My syntax all of a sudden sounds

like Gertrude Stein's syntax. She repeats to have

structure, and profundity. But also to make a

point? I never say "fluids" in the present unless

I am sick. I say Perrier. I could have said

"A Bottle of Perrier" but that is the title of a
short story by Edith Wharton and both she, her story,
and her house The Mount are in the past, about which
I am no longer concerned. I say "plain water," not
"still" or "tap" like they say in expensive restaurants.
I say tea with milk and coffee with hot milk.
I do not say "misto" which means coffee with hot milk
at Starbucks, a chain that sells coffee in the present,
but perhaps not for long the way the economy is going.
The economy is only romantic in the past or the future.
Long-term savings and potential earnings. In the present it sucks.

I have to pee at least two times a night after I go to sleep.
Friends of mine who are much older have told me
that they too have to pee more than one time
each night after they have gone to sleep. This is
an exhausting phenomenon that comes with
having a body in the present. It seems that when
you write about the present you are forced to
write about embarrassing things that the "active"
reader may think self-indulgent. I drink tea before bed.
Chamomile tea. I am not willing to give that up
even to get more rest. It is one of those
little pleasures that keeps the present
from being sheer drudgery. It is not like
the desire for a new coat, which causes
a little leap of hope, and builds up a
micro-story in your head about a different existence,
one in which you wouldn't have to

make up an artificial exercise, an "experiment," in order
to think about the present, because it would "just be."
But the tea is different. The tea is part of
the covert mission of routine. It is almost like religion,
and therefore its withdrawal would likely cause
a reaction that would *seem* unreasonable
and *be* inexplicable. Because tea is *not* religion
even though it has been known to take part
in ceremony. Besides, I don't trust my body
to give up its needs just because I give up mine.

We don't think about having to pee in the past
unless something out of the ordinary happens.
Like peeing when inappropriate, or peeing blood.
Otherwise, it needn't be remembered. I am not
happy that scenes of women peeing are now
included in regular movies as part of "reality."
Men have always peed in movies, because they can
do so anywhere, except in bed, which is a sexual thing
I won't go into here because the "shock value"
of mentioning things like "golden showers"
is a literary provocation that belongs in the past,
because nothing is shocking anymore, except
perhaps the naiveté of people in the past, and
the information they hid from each other
about the basic functions of the body, and
the universal nature of odd desires, and so on.

I have decided to give up on memory. It is too exhausting
and you cannot keep up with it. Every day there is more

of it. And though some things just filter themselves out

naturally, like the memory of all the times you got up

in the middle of the night to pee, other things that seem

irrelevant, and probably are, hang around for a very long time.

In fact, I don't think they *can* go anywhere unless

you experience a head trauma. Therefore it is prudent

to be careful about what gets in. There is much in my

head that I wish weren't. I have not been prudent.

It is difficult to be prudent and live. I will not quote

the William Carlos Williams line that expresses

this sentiment perfectly. It is a line that uses the wisdom

of retrospect, and I am living in the present, not the past.

Besides, I have quoted that line many times now.

I quote it to my students and they give me

a puzzled look. Things I find wise they find puzzling.

I see the wisdom in puzzling things. When supposedly

puzzling things are presented to me they do not seem

puzzling at all, but pleasant. Perhaps because

they are not drab and flat, like the present.

As I write and think about the present,

and try hard not to quote things, which is my

"experiment," it occurs to me that "postmodern fiction"

may just be a fancy word for doing the same.

Even though it is supposedly a pastiche of the past.

Secretly, all fiction writers love the past, but they

are so competitive that when you mention it

they pretend not to know what you are talking about.

Poets are always talking about the past, it is

the *lost grandeur they long for*. Except poets who practice

"new sentences." There was a time when everyone
wrote them. I refused, not because I didn't like
new sentences, I did, but because both the present
and the sentence bored me. Now is my time.
Though this "experiment" is not really creating
new sentences because I refuse to quote things
and new-sentence writers always quoted things.
In fact, that was the core of what they did. They
were not authors, but "quoters." They knew a lot
and quoted things to show their knowledge.
This was not "authority," they rejected "authority."
This is why they refused to think about the self,
it supposedly had too much "authority" in the
Western world. And yet new-sentence writers,
while rejecting the "self," quoted themselves,
as I have done in this "experiment," by repeating
the first line of a stanza, or phrases I've grown fond of,
like "the present is enthusiasm, punctuated every third
day by a minor resistance." Unlike
the new-sentence writers of old, however,
I want authority very badly, but unfortunately
it is not something you can just "get,"
like a new coat when you have the money,
other people must give it to you. Strangely,
people often give authority to writers who make a big show
of being against it, because authority is such an
impressive thing to attack, everyone assumes that
those who do so must really know what they are talking about.

I have decided to give up on memory. It is too exhausting
and you cannot keep up with it. Besides, people hate
complexity. Memory is complicated. Honoring "reality"
is also complex. People hate it. They prefer "ideology."
It is the poet's job to show the "active" reader that
he or she is a dupe of ideology, this lesson is supposed
to feel good, like it feels to get out of prison,
even if you've been in a long time and have no idea
how to rent an apartment or get a job. All these things
are necessities and as such are not supposed to be
fulfilling. But they can be, if you have the right attitude
about the present. Like I do. Did you notice that in
my illustration of how poets who write new sentences
self-quote my own self-quote was a misquote?
The present, no longer resistance, became enthusiasm.
Apparently it is easy to change the habit of relying
on maudlin, complicated memory and compulsive quoting
when writing. It is a question of syntax and grammar.
The body's problems are not so easily remedied.

But the present is just syntax and grammar. I would
quote a long passage from the *Confessions* of St. Augustine
in which he discovers this very fact if my "experiment"
didn't forbid it. Though I have broken my rule
already by self-quoting, just like new-sentence writers.
The present exists but cannot be captured,
except by using the present tense. But even using
the present tense doesn't work. The beginning of this

"experiment," though in the present tense, is now

in the past; the end, tense to be determined, is in the future.

The only true "present" therefore is in the resistance

of each word to meaning in the moment

the "active" reader reads it. Some say this moment

is a kind of writing, where the "active" reader

reconstructs the meaning that I, the writer, had no

control over in the present. They are "free" like a prisoner

released after a long sentence. But it occurs to me

that, though the "active" reader can, caught up

in the enthusiasm of the present, interpret the past,

that is to say the writing, in a way that I in this moment

of the present, or the "active" reader's future,

hadn't accounted for, they are not writing in the

same sense that I am writing. They are reading,

which used to be a highly valued activity in Western

cultures, until it became passive. Now that reading

is passive I must make an effort to distinguish

between the "active" reader and everybody else.

The "active" reader wants my job, they want

to write. They should just do so and leave reading

to those who like to read in the old-fashioned

way. Back when reading was as valued as being frugal.

Like saving up your pennies to buy a new coat

because it is cold outside, not because you have

an idea about fashion and how great you will look

in a new coat. Back when most people would

not drink Perrier or eat filet mignon often enough
to have to think of more than one preparation
for it. There was once a pleasure in repetition too.
Not repetition like you find in the work of Gertrude
Stein, she takes it "way too far," but the repetition
of patterns, like the way the first stanza sets up
certain expectations that the second and third stanzas
conform to. The past really sneaks up on you.
I've been saying "back when" for several sentences
now, ruining my "experiment." I've been tricked
by the past, making it out to be a really great time
with good values. You would think that for artists
who think about "structure," and mock artists
who think about *feeling*, the word "conform,"
from the French meaning "together" and "form,"
would be a positive word. But it isn't. It means
being like other things, which is always interpreted
as not having your own mind, even by people
who are against the idea of having your own mind
because it is self-indulgent. It is a Romantic construct
that is completely beholden to the free market
and therefore exploits working people who are too busy
making ends meet in the present to think about
Perrier, filet mignon, poetry, patterns, and so on.

In fact, if I were an industrial worker
and not a poet and I read this "experiment" I would
think to myself, that poet has too much money,

she has lost touch with working people who
don't care about poetry. It is a vicious cycle.
Bladders and feet, however, are everyone's concern,
culture, education, and class aside. In the present
they press on and pain us. They make me think:
this has got to stop.

THE OPEN SECRET

YIELD: BOUNDLESS SERVINGS

Many cooks shy away from the Divine Mystery of the Universe, for it is rumored to be a difficult dish only experts dare attempt. With this in mind, I have adapted and simplified the old lore to fit the modern homemaker and amateur chef alike. All the ingredients should be readily available on the shelves of any well-stocked American supermarket.

Note: if you have a compromised liver, the recipe may not take.

2 scalene triangles, placed back to back

Energy

A measure of unformed matter

Water (lukewarm)

Dreamlike sense, intuition, apprehension

Dash infernal fire

As many fixed stars as the eye can hold

Flour

Liquid throes of the demiurge*

Preheat oven to the fifth century B.C. Place triangles in energy to soak, while you prepare the other ingredients. Mix water into matter, set aside. Lightly toast dreamlike sense, intuition, and apprehension in a dry skillet until fragrant, then grind in a mortar (if you don't have a mortar, a coffee grinder works just as well). When oven has reached the correct era, add pre-soaked triangles. Check them often, they will multiply very quickly. If

---

*Check the Cosmic Comestibles section of your supermarket. Also available at www.demiurge.com.

they overtake the geometry of your kitchen, you'll have to begin again (see: Solutions to triangle tangles, page 555). Remove triangles from oven, add to matter along with ground spices and dash infernal fire. Toss stars in flour. Fold in. Place all ingredients within the moving image of eternity and swirl gently. Now, for the *pièce de résistance* (you might want to call your guests in to witness the magic): douse in liquid throes, stand back.

From Jennifer Moxley's *Recipes to Impress Abstemious Guests* © Timaeus Publishing Co.

THE VARIOUS SILENCES LIE IN SHADOW

I

Your lyre is muffled with silk, a column of darkness,
A sheltered self, some kind of hell. It follows and dampens
The harkening, *who is singing in the distance?*
I can hear nothing from this shore.

Your lateral movement ensnakes my insight.
O tall tree, who is singing? Down to the ground and then
Up to the heavens where the long-armed archons
Strum rubbery harmonies over the slippery purple

Of my umbrella. Is this darkness or silence?
I hear his feet above my head, impatient besuited
Pacing as he heads purposefully to Lloyds of London,
Followed by skeletons of protected men. Deaf poet,

Who is singing? I can hear nothing, anymore. Is it she?
When weathers of the otherworld fill my ears I hear
Her declaration: the feral grandmother, medusa-gray locks
Lashed in windswept rain as she flouts the too-straight path:

Enfin, on respire!

Vital spirits enter her body and planets play through it.
Then I remember how to breathe, so simple and so rhythmical.
It is said he collected umbrellas to protect against his wounded wife,
Tweedy baffles and ivory handles that deadened the ancient meter.

Thoughtless Orpheus, why did you leave her? Recover the influence.
Let it live. She is the elements, *hear them singing*. I can hear nothing
From this shore. For I'm in the version where you were castrated
By female passion. Take your watery journey, give back

To she who sings (*and knows*). Did you leave her
In search of the solitary, the structural song: no persons?
Perhaps that explains the pleasure we take in rehearsing
The end of things. A city bestrewn with broken

Lyres. Unmuffled and crumpled by bluster. A
Thousand discordant notes. This in the storm
On the way to the opera. But under the lights,
According to Gluck, Eurydice gets to live.

The perfect harmony of Love replaces the broken
Order. Do not run for cover. For *she* is Orpheus.
The hazy spheres spin her song as she sings our
Way toward oneness. Undefended, she will affect us.

II

Let us hear her song. Divers silences under shadow:
Umbrageous forest lit by music to become a sudden
Kingdom of peace. All are welcome. No Zarathustrian
Solitude, no call to quiet meditation. Instead: the dance.

Here is life. And darkness too. The song calls all
To find the center. The stars encandle ravaged branches,
The shabby pelts of starving creatures pattern into
New-made forms. And so through ritual we remember

The cool shelter of this cavern: a vision enlivened beneath
The pleated scallop of my broken umbrella: the spirits of horses
Run beside me. Yet I am alone. Must we be severed
From our true loves to hear their buried voices again?

Under the shelter of another's invention, elements shredded,
Arms bound, my lyre is muffled by silk. O Eurydice, do not stay
Dead, but sing a puncture through this protection,
Remind us of our mistakes. Your harm is not our redemption.

It wounds the gentle covenant: that somehow these signs
Can guide us back to all that we have lost. A concordance of imaged
Spirits moves in the contours of the stone, the godhead's
Message without her: lament without softness or end.

She is metaphor because not mother. Yet without her
There will be no song. No horses running or fires that burn. She is the sign's
Completion. The singing stars have distanced themselves from our
Defeat. Courting the sun of this late millennium Orpheus

Is defenseless. Let him be rejoined to she who sings (*and knows*).
Or are we doomed to lie low? To muddle through the mire
Mumbling songless speech in search of like shapes: to find our way
By facts alone. What evidence do we need? *Listen, someone is*

Singing. A light hums against the deathless sky, night songs
Echo through the dry air: It has finally stopped raining. The singer's
Foot sinks into the sand. Orpheus toys with the threshold.
Will he call her back with a song of regret? Or has a new song

Finally been born? I am wrapped up against the weather, but feel
The centuries beneath my skin. A horse is coming to meet me,
He is unreined and calls my name. His mane is the fibrous lyre
My hands obediently strum. By a touch I am made . . .

III

Boundless, boundless and undone. Must we be severed
From ourselves to sing with the voices of others?
Dismembered by discord: the patterned static of a
Thousand machines speeding through the darkness.

Beneath the hum the gentle strum of a tensed musical
Interval, a repeated ascending arpeggio. Can you hear it
Making its bid to bring the harmony back? The rhetoric
Drowns it. The credentials deaden it. The song will not

Stand before a board of experts. What do they know?
Nothing of what the lion knows, nothing of the chorus
Of touch sung in obedience to stellar logics, orders more
Vast than these small circles confining us with hollow discipline

To the artless dance: an up and a down but no joining.
Thumbed from below we bend at the knees in an ugly
Soulless wobble. Under these reins both Orpheus and
Eurydice court elusive security, are locked in a bank vault

For future study, do not hear the singing and produce
No song. Remember to flout the too-straight path, to
Let the downpour inspire you, to hear the wisdom of the buried
Voices sprouting inside your ear. Those faces in the darkness

Are not an illusion. *Sparagmos*: and he will rejoin Eurydice
In pieces. The notes come free of the staff, the song scatters
As leaves from the branch. Yet these songs cannot be
Lost or depleted. Open your lyre to the sky and catch them.

Rain-pelted, wind-whipped, or sun shining. It makes no difference.
No millennial fears or eschatological dreams. For he did not
Let go or look. And she kept singing that he might know her
As the joyful counterpoint to his mournful song. In the mirror

Of his hair her cryptic smile betrays the memory of death.
Or is it life? What difference? If these patterns we make along
The walls resonate . . . If I reach my hand up and rip the silk
From the skeleton of my umbrella will my body fall out

Of time? Become an instrument, un-citied? If I wrap my arms
Around his neck and smell the earth in his animal warmth
Will the universe fill with music? But wait, it *is* filled, always.
Tuned by his breathing I can hear that singing.

FOYER STATES

I

It was the rain. Thrumming away the months of her locked-up life.
A protectress against the new-made frowns of the power-mad
Disciplinarians. By a woman with money whose father loved her,
Or at least couldn't bear to cut the thread, Hermione, too, was protected.

"Child of Helen and hatred." She did not put a stop to history
But rather remembered it differently. The details. The proprioception
Of the accidental child moving inside her body. The touch of
Vibrating air against her rounded eardrum. Damp hair wound down

The back then wrapped in a towel on a cold afternoon right before
The end of the war. There's a rock in the distance she
Never thought to climb, an ocean that spoke directly to her.
And where is he? Her seemingly private pleasures pain him. How

Could it be so simple? But it was, even for him, who wanted
Nothing more than a selfless caress but felt obliged by official music
To take up the call of battle. Her pleasure offended, given "the times."
Others should be warned. She wandered down the marsh as

He took up the search for martyrs. The ghostly sound of a lonely
Poet who bore the tedium admirably dresses these words
In outdated formality. The existential that would destroy the sensual
Vies with the tyranny of *feeling*. Looks for "meaning." Is it so

Wrong? "I can endow any moment with pathos," she thought. "I am
This privileged and I am this poor. I have forgotten the past, and yet
I am trapped in it. My husband sleeps for years at a time, and when
He's awake he's laughing and grateful. His contentment disrupts

The buried persons shuffling forward to meet me, the portals forced
By dissatisfied energies through which the muffled voices come. Have I
been making them up? I used to hear in every voice the story of
A failed state, a cry of lost potential. That was a mirror of my

Fears. Now I hear something different: more terrifying and more grand.
Who am I to interpret these signs?" Swooning shapes of being leaving
Messages in silt. The ocean's ambivalent song. Even the extraordinary
Life lacks what's needed to take it all in. She sinks back down

Into the fabric and tries to feel consciousness end. Embrace
The rain. She thinks of the anarchy of the aged woman freed
Of all constraint. *Finally, I can breathe!* Just as Hermione climbed the wall
In order to look down on Achilles. She built no workers' utopias in verse

11

To assuage the hatred of having a mind but understood the privilege.
She listened to fate and saw its face: A woman holding a dying soldier.
A lover, a mother, it makes no difference. The solace of woman's flesh
Shredded by pointless death. To hide their murderous exploits experts

Punish the girl. Eurydice bitten into lament. It was her fault.
Her unedited sweetness demanded ending. Aristaeus followed suit.
Loveliness, he believed, must be depleted. The thoughts of a man
(was he really a man?) who caused the death of all his bees.

It was Hermione who told us that when in death Eurydice missed
Only the scent of earth's flowers, had forgotten her husband's song.
Is it true? A gray light, just like the light of this rainy day
Played backdrop to her Elysium. The rain, the rain. But this rain

Is no Elysium, she thought, it is tedious feeling, a banal peace
With the fact of existence. She reached up and felt the box
Around her. It was pliable and warm. A body of air. Is it okay to
Whisper an uplifting message through the hollow substance

Of these walls, even if no one is listening? Someday somebody
Will be. As she heard Hermione singing: the broken voice
Of the diva refusing to leave the stage. Finally alive. Even before
Institutionalized Hermione imagined all handsome young men

Her passionate suitors. She knew herself to be like this: prone to
Dreaming in narratives more fascinating than the facts at hand.
It was as simple as a fringed scarf thrown over the camel back
Of a worn sofa, a blood-orange box with gold detail,

Left on the mantelpiece of a dead fireplace, holding one black
Cigarette. A mirror that could threaten to deflect it. Yet
The damp morning protected the visual frameworks in her mind.
Bookish weather. She remembered a time when every feeling was as palpable

As the chair she was sitting in. They tripped so easily into lyric
Puzzles, jumped over ho-hum grammatical knots. Beautiful patterns
For the ear of the beloved. There was no story that could not be
Altered by the impulse of a moment. Now through the window

The hydrangea waves as if to say: "Just keep still." The bees
And the butterflies will come to you. "But never say *butterfly* in a poem,"
She thought, citing the disciplinarians. Injunctions whispered
In rooms where her poems were being read. Were there really such rooms?

III

Or were they like Hermione's lovers, punctilios lining the outer edges
Of the damaged ego's edifice? Rain slapped the concrete, a wet
Chemical heat. This weather is not willed by the mind, she thought,
Anymore than the sun bleaches and calms because I wish it to do so.

Then she felt a slight dampness in the hair falling down her
Neck. It made her think: *I have made it all up*. As once when
She tried to move the signs an umbrella handed to her by a passing
Stranger suddenly changed into an Orphic lyre. That's when

The singing began. It was as real as Hildegard's conviction that through
The intricate language of image God was speaking directly to her.
Whether it was real or imagined mattered less than the direction
It came from. An object quivering with unrecorded motion.

"The mind needs the world to relieve it of self."
Conversely, "The material world needs the mind simply
to exist." With its removal a break in the current.
An ear without interpreter. An eye all unafraid.

Dream-thrown by the smell of wisteria she will convene
With Hermione in her sleep, await a visitation. She will calculate
The economics of the imagination in the dark and on one hand.
No conjuring of metaphysical content through a heavy literalness

Regarding the day. In her love of essence she is out of fashion.
Artificial light and noise the great threats. Without the various silences
Her thoughts will cower in shadow. Neither shall her nerves know
The sylvan violence that drove us back into the cave, there where

We conjured with a bit of stain the manifold dimensions of being.
Was this before the songs were stifled to stop a siren singing?
"It continues," she thought. This hatred of beauty, of unedited joy.
Why struggle against them? They convince. Just as the floaty

Lillian Gish embodied the way Hester Prynne irked the crabbed soul
Of an entire village by becoming the songbird she chased. Another
Instance of Eurydice's foot pressing the meadow's threshold,
Releasing the intelligence of the sensual, convening with she

Who sings (*and knows*). Hermione channeled Helen not to
Destroy "him" but to see "her" anew. A reversal of the
Typical orbit. The delicate strain of the minor effort echoing
Off ancient bedrock, a song not of *ought to* but of *yes*.

★ ★ ★

NOTES AND ACKNOWLEDGMENTS

The title of the poem "There Is a Birdsong at the Root of Poetry" comes from Robert Duncan's August 22, 1962 letter to Denise Levertov. When I read this line, I became fascinated by the mixed metaphor of a song, usually emanating from on high, being buried, there at the root.

The title "What Was It?" is the same as that of the ghost story by Fitz James O'Brien.

I am grateful to the following editors for publishing some of these poems as limited-edition chapbooks: Alan Felsenthal and Ben Estes for "Coastal" (Song Cave); Karen Randall for "Evacuations" (Least Weasel); and Daniel Poppick and Rob Schlegel for "The Various Silences Lie in Shadow" and "Foyer States," which they published together as *Foyer States* (Catenary).

I am also grateful to the magazines and journals that published versions of some of these poems: *The Brooklyn Rail, Colorado Review, Court Green, Gulf Coast, The Iowa Review, A Public Space, Sixth Finch, Vanitas,* and *VQR.* The poem "The Open Secret" was written for the artist Suzanne Bocanegra's "Recipe Card" project, published in *Esopus* magazine.